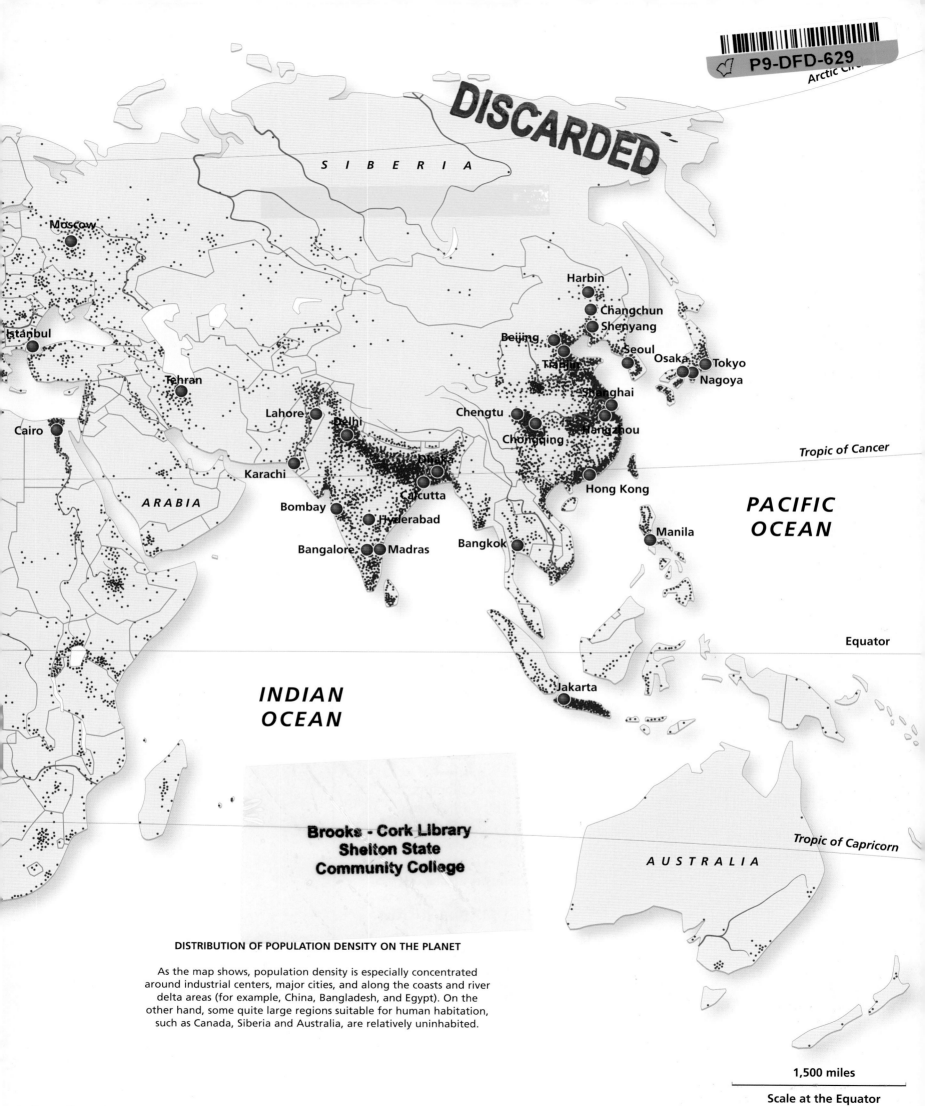

SIBERIA

Arctic Circle

Moscow

Harbin

Changchun

Shenyang

Istanbul

Beijing

Seoul

Tianjin

Osaka

Tokyo

Nagoya

Tehran

Shanghai

Lahore

Delhi

Chengtu

Hangzhou

Cairo

Chongqing

**PACIFIC
OCEAN**

Tropic of Cancer

Karachi

Dhaka

ARABIA

Calcutta

Bombay

Hyderabad

Hong Kong

Bangalore

Madras

Bangkok

Manila

**INDIAN
OCEAN**

Equator

Jakarta

Tropic of Capricorn

AUSTRALIA

DISTRIBUTION OF POPULATION DENSITY ON THE PLANET

As the map shows, population density is especially concentrated
around industrial centers, major cities, and along the coasts and river
delta areas (for example, China, Bangladesh, and Egypt). On the
other hand, some quite large regions suitable for human habitation,
such as Canada, Siberia and Australia, are relatively uninhabited.

1,500 miles

Scale at the Equator

A R C T I C A

Library of Congress Cataloging-in-Publication Data

Dubois, Philippe J.
[Avenir de la terre. English]
Earth from above : sustainable development in a changing world / text by
Philippe J. Dubois and Valérie Guidoux ; adapted by Robert Burleigh ;
drawings by Sylvia Bataille.
p. cm.
Includes index.
ISBN 0-8109-5018-9
1. Sustainable development—Juvenile literature. 2. Human geography—
Juvenile literature. 3. Environmental degradation—Juvenile litèerature. 4.
Aerial photography—Juvenile literature. I. Guidoux, Valérie. II. Burleigh,
Robert. III. Bataille, Sylvia, ill. IV. Title.

HC79.E5D8313 2004
338.9'27—dc22
2004003144

Printed and bound in Belgium
10 9 8 7 6 5 4 3 2 1

Harry N. Abrams, Inc.
100 Fifth Avenue
New York, NY 10011
www.abramsbooks.com

Abrams is a subsidiary of

LA MARTINIÈRE

Yann Arthus-Bertrand

THE FUTURE OF THE EARTH

An Introduction to Sustainable Development for Young Readers

Adapted by
Robert Burleigh

Text by
Philippe J. Dubois
and Valérie Guidoux

Drawings by
Sylvia Bataille

HARRY N. ABRAMS, INC., PUBLISHERS

How to explore this book:

The Future of the Earth has been organized to highlight the diversity, richness, and complexity of sustainable development issues around the globe. Each page presents another part of the world and the global concerns which impact on it, and, the authors hope, the beginning of solutions to the many problems our planet faces. Looking at these issues thematically adds another dimension to the ongoing discussion. Therefore, the contents of the book may also be explored through the themes provided below.

When you're young, it can be hard to imagine how things used to be.

At the age of ten or twelve, you probably haven't lived through a great number of changes. But just ask your grandfather, your grandmother, or your great-grandmother—they'll remember very clearly that taking an airplane was a real adventure when they were children. There were far fewer cars on the road, no one had walked on the moon, and space rockets and satellites were something out of science fiction!

In the span of a single century, science and technology have progressed at a dizzying speed. So fast, in fact, that we have not fully understood how all of these changes in transportation, communication, industrial production, agriculture, and other fields have affected the earth.

But little by little, we realized that petroleum, which makes airplanes fly and cars run, pollutes the atmosphere. Also, the intensive harvesting of forests makes the production of books and newspapers possible—but we have seen it obliterate the plants and animals that live in those environments.

There are many similar examples. Nature's balance has been shattered. We know today that our planet's climate is changing as a result of human activity. This transformation is a matter of concern for everyone, including farmers in Madagascar whose lands are losing their rich soil, inhabitants of Tokyo who have trouble breathing, fishermen who net smaller catches, and vacationers in colder areas who complain that winter snows no longer fall.

All of these problems and changes gave birth to the idea of "sustainable development." This unwieldy term describes our attempts to balance the needs of modern life with the treatment that our planet can handle. It is no easy task.

Politicians are beginning to embrace this idea; that's why, in our time, the various heads of state meet regularly to discuss it. Gradually (but much too slowly) steps are being taken to repair past mistakes and prepare the way to the future—for example, by reducing greenhouse gases that contribute to climate change. Often, though, we witness more speeches than action.

Well then, it's up to every one of us to get busy.

Some citizens are launching initiatives that affect their local areas. Even though the work that remains is enormous, each effort matters: sorting waste products, reducing our use of cars, protecting natural environments, buying only environmentally friendly products, and others.

Sustainable development means, too, an awareness that the world's riches are unevenly distributed. The basic needs of life, which we take for granted, cannot be provided everywhere: having enough to eat, safe water, and schools and medical resources available . . .

Today, 20% of the Earth's inhabitants share 80% of the world's riches. You're probably included in this 20%. But what about the others? It's time we think about them so that, together, we can guarantee the Earth's future.

—Hervé de La Martinière

The greenhouse effect

The illustration on the left helps describe the greenhouse effect. Earth's atmosphere lets a portion of the sun's rays pass through. The ground absorbs one-half of these rays (1). The other half are reflected back out into space by clouds or absorbed by the atmosphere (2). Meanwhile, Earth emits its own heat in the form of infrared radiation, some of which escapes into space (3). The atmosphere (4) and gases that exist naturally, such as water vapor and carbon dioxide, intercept the rest of the radiation. Just as a garden greenhouse does, these gases send the trapped heat back to Earth, making the temperature here just right for life to flourish.

So what's the problem? In a simple phrase, things are heating up. Human activity, especially manufacturing and transportation, discharges more and more "greenhouse gases" (carbon dioxide, methane, and nitrous oxide). These gases form an increasingly substantial layer in the atmosphere, which reflects back more heat to Earth than ever. Scientists believe that in the next one hundred years, the temperature may increase as much as 4 to 7 degrees F, transforming climates worldwide.

Abundant crops deplete the land

Wheat (above) and grapevines (below) dominate this landscape in southwestern France. The lone tree in the center suggests that perhaps a long hedgerow once grew here.

Since 1950, intensive farming practices have severely harmed nearly 40% of our planet's cultivated land.

Whether you visit a farm in Iowa or southwestern France, chances are the landscape will look much the same: Wheat fields next to corn fields next to soy beans next to beets. Why do these farms look like they were made with the same cookie cutter?

Most wealthy countries have expanded the practice of "intensive farming." In a nutshell, this means cultivating large crops over vast areas with minimal labor to produce high crop yields. But to farm in this way, you need to use advanced technology, huge machines, and chemicals (including pesticides and fertilizers that stimulate sprouting). Unfortunately, these machines discharge greenhouse gases, such as carbon dioxide and methane. And fertilizer nitrates combined with pesticides filter down into the earth and pollute the fresh water reserves underneath. Pesticides can also poison insects, such as bees and butterflies—and the birds that eat them. If that weren't enough, some crops (corn, for example) drink up lots of water. Yes, intensive farming may yield abundant harvests—but at what cost to the environment?

We can do better! To feed people in the future, we'll need to pollute less while farming and preserve Earth's limited resources—including water reservoirs, overused soil that is losing nutrients, and endangered species.

Say good-bye to the wild

In their eagerness to acquire ever more land to farm, agricultural businesses often destroy wetlands, forests, or hedgerows (as in the example you see here) that stand in their way. But these habitats are home to many native plants and animals, which may become endangered or die away altogether. There's a chain reaction: The wind, which more and more encounters no obstacles, speeds up water evaporation, which dries up the fields. This in turn causes rainwater to run off instead of sinking into the ground where it can replenish the plants that live there.

Coral reefs under assault . . .

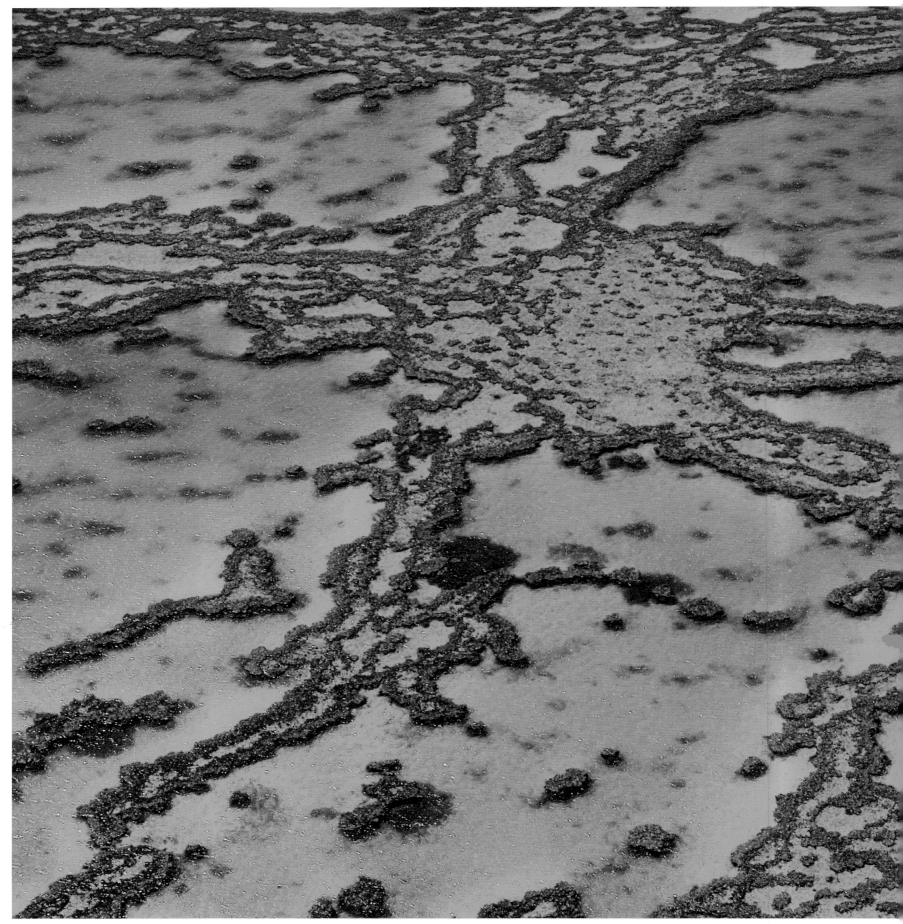

As far as the eye can see, the Great Barrier Reef of Queensland, Australia, invites divers. But scientists are worried. Why? Because of pollution and increased temperatures, the coral is deteriorating rapidly and losing its ability to grow.

Right now, more than one-half of all the world's coral reefs are threatened.

How wonderful the coral reef is, whether you're gazing at the top of it (as in this photograph) or studying its underwater beauty. Corals are marine structures formed over time by a combination of algae and polyps (tiny animals). Many varieties of sea life—fish, sea anemones, sponges, jellyfish, and crustaceans of all kinds—call the coral reef home.

In the Australian Great Barrier Reef, which extends over nearly 1,250 miles, thousands of species live side by side. Tourists flock here to dive into the heart of this ocean of life—but perhaps not for much longer. Here's why. The coral reef is, in fact, among the most threatened natural environments on the planet. In some spots, pollution is destroying the fragile corals. In others places, divers damage the reef. But you won't guess what poses one of the greatest threats: heat!

Increased temperatures are endangering the coral reefs. In warmer waters, the algae connected to the coral die. Then, in a kind of chain reaction, life leaches out of the coral, bleaching it. And the coral reef as we knew it is no more.

Year after year, the deluge . . .

Floodwaters engulf a house near Dhaka, Bangladesh. Luckily, the people in this densely populated nation have adapted to the flood conditions. But as the climate changes more rapidly, the floods become harder to predict.

From the 1980s to the 1990s, the number of people worldwide affected by natural disasters rose by 50%.

Look down—do you see the man with the little girl? Do you think they're happy to be surrounded by swirling, muddy water? Not likely! Here in Bangladesh, the monsoon season unleashes torrential rains on the region for several months. Rivers swollen by water tumble down from the Himalaya Mountains, making the flooding even worse.

The people who live here have adapted their lives to the deluge. For instance, do you notice the long shafts of bamboo laid lengthwise? These allow people to at least stay above the raging torrent! But for how long? Well, these floods are getting bigger every year. And again, climatic changes play a role, disrupting air mass circulation and pulling in stronger storms and rains. During the decade of the 1990s, each monsoon season killed more people than the last.

What to do? The answer is to attempt to prevent these floods by building dikes and setting up effective warning systems. In Dhaka, the Bangladeshi capital, such steps have saved several hundred lives since 2001. As one national official remarked: "One dollar spent on flood prevention means four dollars saved on flood assistance."

Some worrying numbers

Catastrophic floods worldwide have increased dramatically. Just do the numbers yourself—six major floods during the decade of the 1950s, seven during the 1960s, eight during the 1970s, eighteen during the 1980s, and twenty-six during the past decade! From 1971 to 1995, floods affected the lives of 1.5 billion people throughout the world. Of these, nearly 318,000 died by drowning and more than 81 million emerged homeless and without shelter. Of course, underdeveloped countries with fewer hospitals and less organized aid had more victims than wealthy nations.

New species, new problems . . .

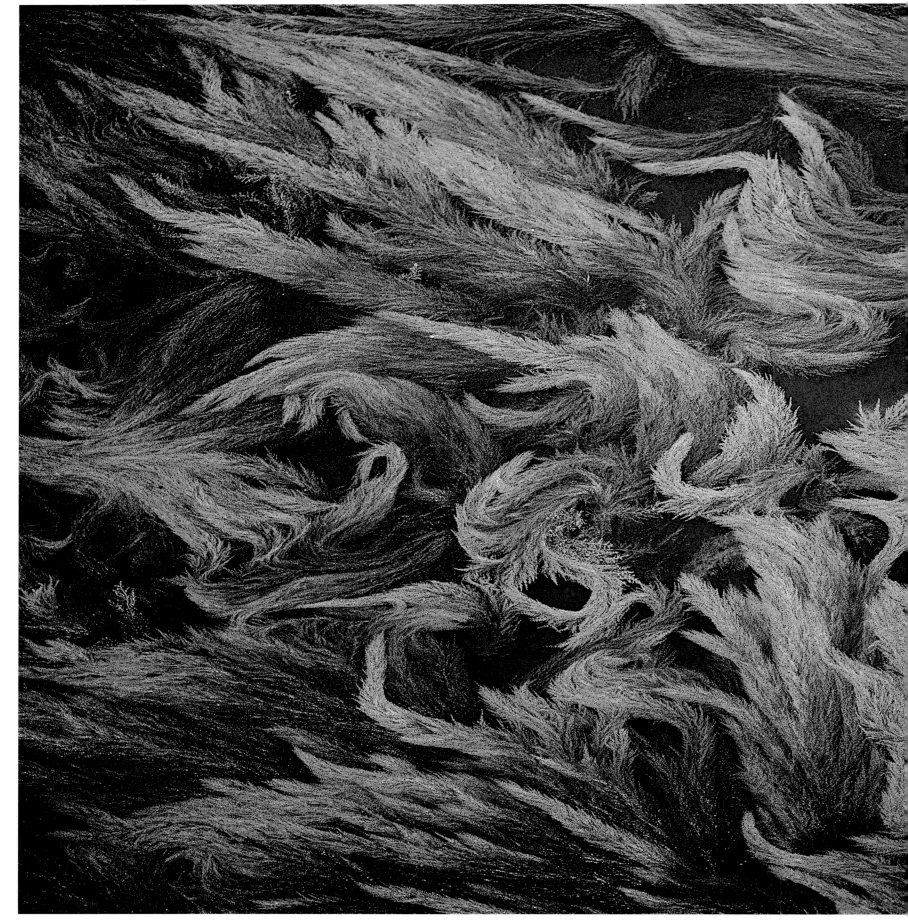

The large mass of seaweed you see here, which was introduced into the waters off the coast of France, is being watched by scientists: if it propagates too rapidly, it could damage other types of seaweed and marine animals. Fortunately—at the moment—its spread appears to be contained.

Newly introduced, or alien, species have caused damage amounting to billions of dollars each year.

It may be interesting to introduce plant or animal species into a new environment. But take care. For example, water hyacinths floating in a small garden pool look quite harmless, don't they? It's hard to believe that if such pretty flowers proliferate in canals and rivers where they don't belong, they can stop small boats in their tracks and smother other nearby living things!

From the moment we humans started traveling the world, we've taken some undesirable "guests" along. Exhibit 1: the rat. Rats hitched a ride with us to anywhere and everywhere and, on at least some Pacific islands, have driven to extinction many plants and birds that once lived there. In fact, dozens of plants and animals have been set loose in places they were never meant to live, wreaking havoc on their new environment.

Often these invaders increase their numbers by leaps and bounds, threatening to overcome the local species. Think of the Florida turtle. Released into European waterways, this turtle now threatens other tortoises native to the region, such as the European Pond Terrapin.

Government agencies, of course, are responding to these unwanted invasions. The agencies often attempt to remove the alien organisms and reestablish the native environment—but this is not always easy, and the cost is high.

A species once introduced for its fur, the muskrat has invaded the rivers and ponds of Europe. And look at what has happened. Today muskrat burrows often make embankments and dikes crumble.

People forced to leave home . . .

The 1999 conflict in Kosovo caused many Albanians living in that Serbian province to flee. When they reached Albania, 400,000 people took refuge in tent camps like this one.

Sad to say, there are about 20.6 million refugees in the world.

Does this tent city look like your town? Can you imagine how it would feel to have to leave your home forever with only the clothes you are wearing, with no idea of where you would sleep that night? For many people, this is no idle question. It is a harsh reality. When war and disaster strike, men, women, and children are forced to flee just to survive. We call these people refugees. And there are nearly 21 million of them throughout the world.

People moving or fleeing, and thus becoming refugees, didn't start in the twentieth century. It has been going on throughout human history. Many Irish people were forced to leave their country due to famine in the nineteenth century. Vietnamese and Cambodians left their war-wracked countries in the 1970s. And some people, such as the Palestinians, remain refugees living in tent cities for many years.

Future events will no doubt force more people to take to the roads. Our century will most certainly add "climate-driven" refugees, people driven out by floods and other disasters. Should they be pressed to return home at any cost, or should they receive the assistance they need to begin a new life elsewhere? This question remains an unanswered one. Children and grandchildren of refugees today contribute to the wealth of many countries. At the same time, though, their courage and energy are missed by the countries they leave behind.

Slowly but surely, the desert advances

The many wells of Araouane, a village in Mali located about 150 miles north of Timbuktu, once attracted caravan drivers and nomads. Today, the sands have swallowed everything.

Once-good land now becoming desert affects more than 1 billion human beings around the world.

You can almost taste the dry sand engulfing everything in its path. This small village of Araouane in northern Mali could not withstand the advancing desert.

"Desertification" is a hard word to say, but an easy one to understand: the drying up of the land. Nearly everywhere in the world the desert is advancing, especially in arid regions like parts of Africa. Climate change certainly does nothing to help the situation, but other things also contribute to the problem. First, there's deforestation (another big word). When people cut down all the trees, nothing is left to stop the sand or winds that sweep along the ground. What happens then? The sand and winds carry off the most fertile soil layers. Along with that, intensive farming exhausts the land, and chemical fertilizers and pollution degrade it.

Think of this: In China, the desert is creeping toward Beijing at the rate of slightly more than a mile per year. When the land dries up and becomes desert, land suitable for farming recedes. Farmers often have to leave their farms and look elsewhere for land or for other work.

But in some cases the desert's stranglehold may be only temporary. Drought follows the laws of the climatic cycle: one drenching rainy season and—who knows?—harvests might be good again. Beyond this, people can also help fight the growth of the desert. How? Well, two good starts would be to avoid deforestation and use farming techniques that don't require huge amounts of water.

Sand is gradually overwhelming vines like these, making the soil appear yellow.

Creating fairer trade

Children in rich countries will eat the pineapples harvested here, in the Ivory Coast. Pineapple growers from South America and Hawaii are also competing in a price war, causing pineapple prices to spiral downward. But the growers' living depends on selling these delicious fruits.

During the harvest season in Kenya, 30% of the coffee pickers are children.

Fair is fair. But who decides? Take Max Havelaar, a Dutchman who protested against the injustices of the coffee trade as long ago as 1860. What was he so mad about? At that time, after buying coffee from the Indonesians, coffee merchants habitually sold it in Europe at a price so low that the Indonesian farmers could barely survive. This certainly wasn't fair to the farmers—then or now. And Havelaar wasn't forgotten. In 1988, Havelaar's name began appearing on bags of coffee sold under the "fair trade" label. But just what does fair trade mean?

On the international market, wholesale buyers try to pay as little as possible for basic foods such as cocoa, coffee, pineapple, and sugar. Nothing wrong with trying to get a good price, right? Everyone looks for sales when they're shopping! It's easy to forget the poverty of the many people who, whether here or at the opposite end of the globe, make what we buy. Well, fair trade attempts to help us remember these people. Some groups in richer countries have decided to buy coffee and other products at a somewhat higher price. By giving up the lowest price, they help these poor farmers make a better living and obtain more social benefits, such as medicine and education. When we in turn buy these "fair traded" products, we become links in a chain that enhances the living conditions of millions of small-scale producers throughout the world.

Great cities—but not great air . . .

Nearly 11 million people live in and around Paris, France. Every day, 3 million vehicles enter and leave the city, which has a hard time dealing with all the traffic! In the distance, a layer of yellowish air—pollution—blights the blue sky.

Look out above—and below! In the next ten years, car pollution could increase by 25%.

How many people do you think live and work in the vast number of buildings you see in this picture? That's right—millions! Cities are exciting—throngs of people, glittering lights, stores that sell anything you can imagine. By the year 2020, one-third of us will be living in cities with more than 1 million inhabitants—and we'll also probably be breathing dirty air!

Whether it's in New York, London, Tokyo, or Paris, cars cause 80% of air pollution. And the intense heat of summer just makes things worse. That's when polluting gases can completely enclose a city in a cocoon of smog. And because climate changes multiply the number of hot days, this is happening more often, bringing higher numbers of breathing and heart-related problems. But traffic is not the only cause. Factories and heating plants near the cities also pollute our atmosphere.

What can be done? Some major cities, such as Berlin, New York, and Stockholm, have carved out large green spaces, or parks, that act as "lungs" to help decrease the effects of pollution.

Cities are wonderful places, but you have to be able to breathe! How can we reduce air pollution? Here's one suggestion: what about taking public transportation instead of driving to reduce the number of vehicles on the road? Buses, subways, and bicycles are great alternatives.

Sticking together helps—and hurts

Eldey Island, in Iceland, forms the nesting ground for thousands of gannets, which return there every spring. The two surviving great auks were killed on this island in 1844.

One of four mammals, 12% of all birds, one-third of all fish, and, probably, more than half of all flowering plants and insects are endangered.

Do you see those tiny white dots covering the rock like confetti? Believe it or not, these "dots" are really birds. Tens of thousands of gannets have flocked to this small island in Iceland to reproduce—a bird colony that is among the largest on Earth.

Living in a group improves the birds' chances to find abundant feeding grounds and keep predators at bay. If a falcon came along looking for a quick meal, it would have trouble fending off the counterattacks of thousands of gannets! And the sheer walls of the island make it hard for predators to gain a claw hold. Ideal habitats like this one are rare, so these birds, like sea otters, sea lions, and others elsewhere, gather here in great numbers.

Yet these large numbers also represent a possible weakness. A single disaster caused by pollution or a food shortage would strike thousands of birds at once. For instance, higher water temperatures and over-fishing can lead to the decline of whole species of fish. This happened in the North Atlantic in the late 1960s, when the herring population almost entirely disappeared, and again in the mid-1980s, when the population of capelin declined. Both events seriously hurt the fishing trade. Water pollution can also kill off large segments of these closely packed colonies. So as you see, "sticking together" has a plus side—but a minus side, too.

Seeing beyond the tip of one's island . . .

Protecting various small natural paradises allows the plants and animals living there to survive. But it's not enough. On a wider scale, it's important to conserve the seas, forests, and mountains that harbor these beautiful environments. Creating reserves and parks is fine, but it is also necessary to stop the uncontrolled exploitation of the habitats that surround them.

Day by day, the ice melts away

The Perito Moreno glacier pours into Lake Argentino in Patagonia, in southern Argentina. The shrinking of South American glaciers has quickened since the 1990s.

Over twenty thousand square miles of ice, a surface area nearly the size of West Virginia, disappear each year.

This superb Patagonian glacier ends its slow journey in the clear waters of a lake. But will it still exist in fifty—or in twenty—years? That's the question that scientists are asking as they watch the world's glaciers melt like ice cream on a hot day.

Glaciers follow natural cycles. But many of them have been losing surface area for several decades. Gas discharges combined with human industry are causing an overall temperature increase all over the globe. These higher temperatures trigger climate changes that speed the ice-melting process. Some glaciers, such as those on Mt. Kilimanjaro in Tanzania, decreased rapidly. Most Alaskan glaciers have also lost volume in the recent past.

Melted ice reaching the sea accounts for a small portion (about 20%) of the ocean's rise. At the same time, glaciers melting in the Himalayas raise the threat of floods nearby. Glacial lakes can fill to flood level and then overflow, dumping their excess water into densely populated areas. Water is one of humanity's great gifts—except when there is too much of it!

Look out—we're under attack!

You're looking down on an invasion of locusts near Ranohira, Madagascar. People have always lived with insect infestations. Today, our task is to find ways of curbing them, while at the same time preserving the environment.

Concentrations of pesticides in gardens are even higher than in cultivated croplands.

It looks like a huge dark cloud, but it's something much worse. Spreading over miles and miles, a swarm of billions of locusts swoops down to devour the vegetation below, including crops! Since the dawn of time, the African continent has periodically suffered infestations of these insects, which resemble huge grasshoppers.

People have resorted to insecticides to kill the locusts. The insecticides work, but the insects are not the only victims. Insecticides (such as DDT, which is now banned in many countries) also kill the surrounding wildlife, especially animals that feed on insects. And these chemicals don't go away—they stay in the environment and in the animals that ingest them.

Pesticides are a dangerous source of soil and water pollution. As an alternative, people are trying to come up with some natural weapons in the fight against destructive bugs. One example: a spray that consists of a microscopic fungus that clings to the locust's body and grows on its insides, finally killing it. And a bacterium that can destroy butterflies that eat cotton and corn shoots. Such natural methods are promising. After all, using insecticides on a massive scale not only pollutes, but gradually becomes less and less effective. Why is that? Because the targeted organisms often develop immunity to these chemicals over time!

Nuclear energy: productive, but dangerous

Until 1986, fifty thousand people lived in Pripyat. But then came the Chernobyl plant disaster. Total evacuation followed. All around the city, nature was severely affected: trees withered away, and people and animals were born deformed.

In 2002, 441 nuclear reactors in 32 countries produced highly radioactive, long-lived waste products, which continue to accumulate at storage sites.

April 26, 1986, was a day like any other—until the explosion of Reactor No. 4 at the Chernobyl nuclear plant in Ukraine. The explosion created a terrible catastrophe. A radioactive cloud blanketed a large part of Europe.

What, you may ask, is radioactivity, anyway? It's invisible pollution that shatters the structure of the cells that make up all living things, from microbes to you! Radioactivity can cause serious illnesses—and especially cancers—years, or even dozens of years, after its release. Several million people suffered the after-effects of the Chernobyl explosion—first and foremost, the people who lived nearby.

The nuclear industry generates electricity from one specific metal: uranium. Many countries obtain a large percentage of their power from nuclear plants. Unlike petroleum and coal, this kind of energy doesn't worsen the greenhouse effect. But watch out—it must be handled very carefully! And this productive yet terribly dangerous energy creates another problem: nuclear waste stays radioactive for centuries, and even millennia. We must store it in a way that doesn't endanger our children and grandchildren. For now, we bury nuclear waste deep in the earth or under the sea, in thick concrete cases. But is this the best solution? Unfortunately, no one quite knows.

Can we live together?

In this village near Bandiagara in Mali, the houses are clustered on land-grant plots where each family lives. The people dry their harvests on their terraces, and each plot has its own granary for millet.

Thousands of groups throughout the world work hard on behalf of their district, their city, or the planet as a whole.

Looks peaceful, doesn't it? Under these roofs, the Dogon culture, one of the most ancient in Africa, is still going strong. Here, as in some other parts of the world, the traditional way of life has preserved remarkable cooperation among villagers and within families. It's hard to believe, but for the Dogon people, words such as "poverty" and "orphan" have no meaning.

The Dogons have found a way to live in harmony with nature. You can see this reflected in the landscape itself: in the houses made of earth and the crops encircling the villages. But nothing is absolutely secure. The smallest event can change everything. Poor harvests, young people leaving for the cities, or political disturbances and war can upset this fragile balance forever.

Indeed, change will probably come. But we can hope that in the future, traditional communities such as this one will have the opportunity to adapt to the best development practices—such as those relating to health and education—the modern world offers.

Tourism—good or bad?

Throughout the world, remote areas that have escaped industrial development are today considered treasures. Many city dwellers love to commune with nature in remote wilderness areas, often in the developing world. But tourists have a responsibility, too. They must respect these environments and the local culture to help preserve traditional ways of life while providing income to the regions' inhabitants.

Many ways to catch a fish . . .

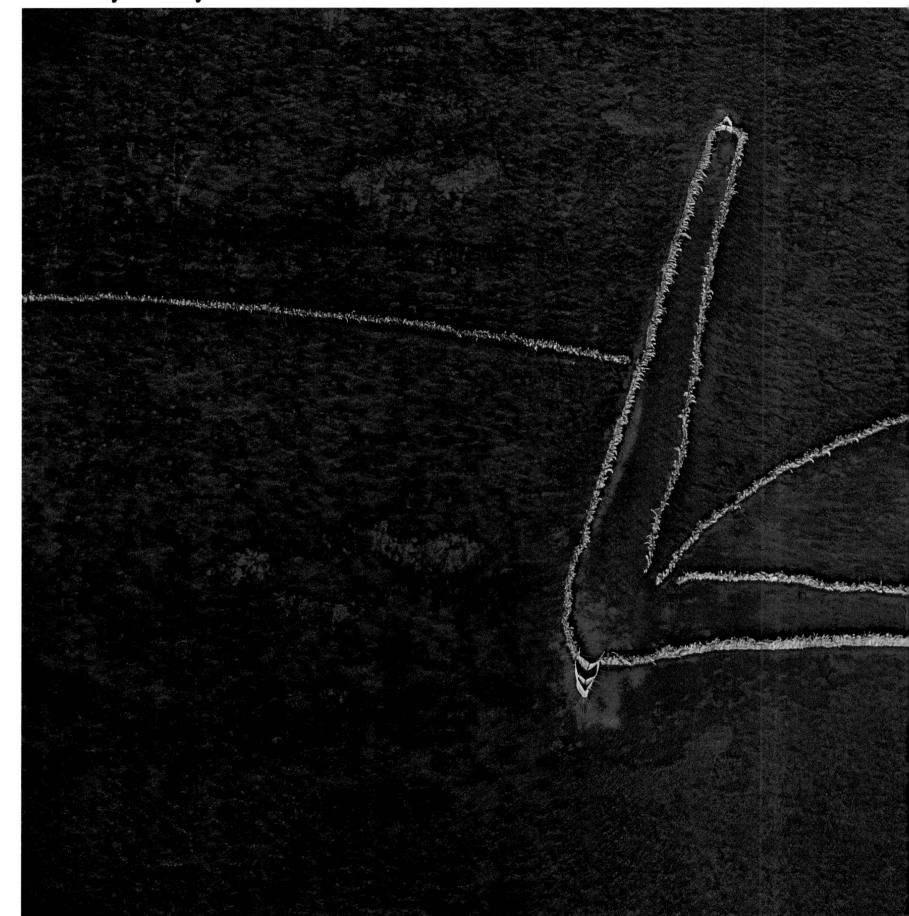

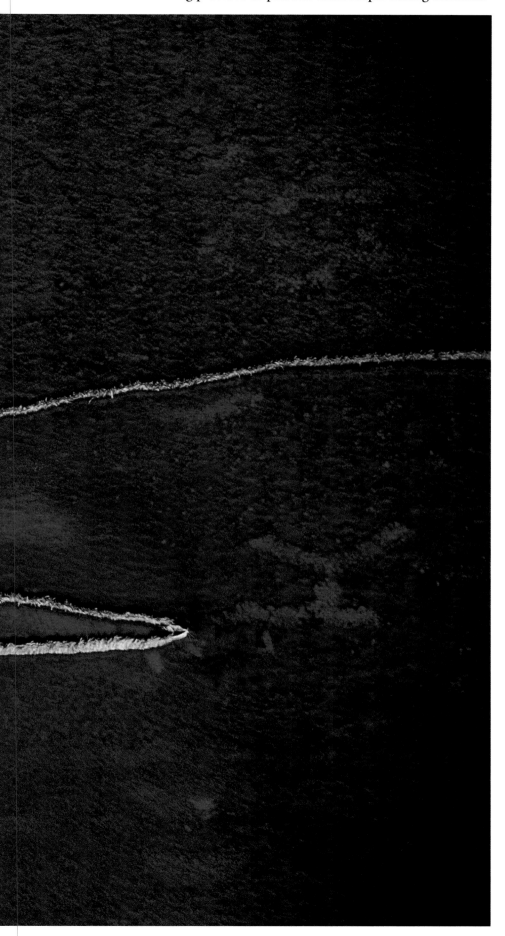

Barriers woven of palm fronds herd fish toward a trap. Off the coast of Tunisia, this traditional fishing method holds down the size of the catch. These days, financial assistance is being provided to preserve such simple fishing methods.

Industrialized fishing of big fish, such as cod and halibut, has depleted fish stocks by 80%.

No, this picture's not a drawing of a boomerang or the letter L! It's just a traditional way of catching fish—but catching them in smaller numbers.

Oceans are large, abundant, and teeming with fish, right? Although we may see oceans as inexhaustible food reserves, this is no longer true. During the twentieth century, fishing changed from a trade practiced by skilled people who fished only for what they needed to a large-scale industry. Factory ships with gigantic nets now travel the oceans, catching tons of fish each year (around 90 million tons, to be more exact).

Despite the effectiveness of present-day fishing methods, catches are decreasing. Big fish populations, such as cod, are experiencing a severe decline (down by 80% during the last fifteen years). Some species might not even survive.

Why are the fish in danger? Ocean pollution from hydrocarbons (petroleum) poisons fish and the animals that eat them. And the bigger nets companies use don't just capture fish—they also scoop up tortoises, dolphins, and sea birds, including the albatross, whose numbers are falling sharply.

The solution is simple, but painful. We need to reduce corporate fishing. Relying more on fish farms could help preserve the fish stock. This would, of course, affect people, too—but the fate of the oceans' riches hangs in the balance.

The wages of war . . .

You're looking at B-52 bombers lined up at a military base in the United States. America spends three dollars per citizen per day on weapons. At the same time, 1.2 billion people throughout the world live on less than one dollar a day.

Governments all over the globe spend almost fifteen times more on weapons than on aid to poor nations.

The planes in this photograph are not toys. They are designed to drop bombs and fly only at times of war. And listen to this: Right now people are fighting in as many as fifty different conflicts in various parts of the world. Even when the fighting is finally over, war's destruction leaves after-effects. In fact, war often goes hand-in-hand with poverty. That's because a country involved in a conflict is usually more concerned about getting weapons and soldiers than about building schools, farming the land, and preparing its citizens for the future.

It gets worse. In wartime people destroy without caring about the human and ecological consequences. In 1990, for example, the Iraqi army sabotaged an oil terminal in Kuwait, allowing 800,000 tons of petroleum to pour into the sea. Bombs, chemical weapons, and anti-personnel landmines (explosives buried in roadways and fields) kill and maim thousands of people every year.

War can severely damage the economy. But guess who makes a lot of money during war? Arms merchants, of course! In 2000, expenditures on weapons rose to $750 billion. And after the war ends? Countries that sell arms often profit from the contracts for reconstruction projects—projects caused by the very war itself!

Soil crumbles into dust . . .

On the island of Madagascar, the river carries off red soil to the sea. This is fertile soil now lost to farming. The result? Problems increase for farmers who want to grow and sell their crops.

The soil covering nearly one-half of African lands is gradually losing fertility.

Have you ever seen such an odd red river? But the photograph doesn't lie. Here is what's happening: This Madagascan river carries off silt—dirt that falls straight downward from the hills that border the river. What remains are hills completely stripped bare, hills where nothing at all will grow.

In recent decades, people living here have cut down the trees to use for building materials, for heating, and to make way for additional farmland. But alas, trees are what held the soil in place. You can see for yourself the sad results.

Farmers who grow crops on slopes often clear land to increase their farming area. But with no trees to hold down the soil, heavy rains, especially in tropical regions, can cause deadly landslides. In some places, soil rushes down steep hills and destroys whole villages. Each year, thousands of people die in this way, buried in huge mudslides.

It's only *after* they've cleared too much land that people finally understand—if it's not too late!—that they have to preserve the vegetation to prevent erosion from sweeping away the valuable soil.

Feeding the world—the *gaucho* way

Argentinian *gauchos*, or cowboys, herd their cattle across a river. These cattle, which are grown for slaughter, graze nearby on pastureland. This is called non-intensive breeding. Intensive breeding calls for raising cattle in buildings, on concrete floors.

By 2020, the earth will have to feed an additional 1.5 billion inhabitants.

Is raising cattle the best way to use the land? Good question. About 800 million people in the world suffer from malnutrition. Many countries don't grow enough to feed their population and haven't the resources to buy food. At the same time, these same countries sometimes use their land in part to grow crops for export! This was Sudan's case in 1989. At the same time that the Sudanese population was facing possible famine, the country was exporting thousands of tons of groundnuts and sorghum that went to feed European cattle. What gives?

In terms of land usage, feeding a single person with a steak is equivalent to feeding five or six people with rice or wheat. But in wealthy countries, people eat meat almost every day, so farmers raise lots of cattle, poultry, and hogs. The result is that we use more than one-third of the grain we grow to feed animals, rather than people!

In 2020, our planet will be home to nearly 8 billion people. To feed that many, humans will probably have to consume less meat so that we can grow more crops in the countries whose people will need them. Only in this way can we make sure that everyone has enough to eat.

Trees: going, going, gone?

You might think this is a small island of trees in a sea of cereal crops. But it's actually a part of the forest of Mato Grosso do Norte in Brazil, which has suffered the ravages of the chain saw.

Each year, over fifty thousand square miles of forestland disappear throughout the world.

What happened to the trees that once would have filled this photograph? They are gone, cut down because forests are an important economic resource for developing countries. In fact, every hour across our planet, seven football fields' worth of forestland are destroyed. At that rate, how many of these forests will still be standing after a few more decades? Probably not too many!

Concern over our disappearing forestlands is more than a concern with tropical beauty. Forests are the lungs of the planet. You might say that forests breathe for us! Here's how. Forests give off oxygen and absorb some of the excess carbon dioxide that we produce. Along with this, tropical forests are home to amazing animals and plants as well as people who have lived there for centuries.

Fortunately, in some places the story is different. In Europe and North America, forests are doing well. Thanks to well-managed forestry, we are learning to avoid random, unplanned cutting. But there is still much more work to be done. Let's hope that sustainable forest development will soon become a reality everywhere.

Once cleared, the Mato Grosso forest gives way to fields of wheat and soybeans, which are used to feed livestock in other parts of the world.

IVORY COAST, AFRICA

Water, water, everywhere? Not quite

The average American uses more than 150 gallons of water per day; the average European, more than 60 gallons; but an average African, only around 8. Here, near Doropo in the Ivory Coast, the water that people draw from the well is a very precious resource.

Each year, worldwide, unhealthy water causes 5 million deaths.

How do you get your water? Maybe you just go over to the faucet and turn it on. But imagine what it would be like to have to search for your own water every day. Do you see these bowls lined up single file? They are waiting to be filled with drinking water. Here in Africa, as in other hot places, finding water for drinking, washing, and farming is a daily struggle. It's hard to believe, but throughout the world, more than 1 billion people have little access to drinkable water.

As a vital resource, water has become a major political issue. In some places, rivers and lakes overlap several countries. This fact has sometimes started conflicts in regions where water is scarce—for instance, in Turkey, Syria, and Iraq. The Tigris and Euphrates Rivers rise in Turkey, where dams built to store water have lowered the water's flow rate for Turkey's neighbors.

Around the world, crop irrigation accounts for 70% of fresh water use, and unfortunately many present-day irrigation systems waste water. However, people are trying to find solutions to this problem. In some arid countries, such as Israel and the United Arab Emirates, researchers have invented drip systems that use minimal water amounts. In this way, vegetables such as cucumbers and tomatoes use only the amount of water they need. And here is another partial solution: to deal with water shortages, farmers in some places are experimenting with sturdier varieties of plants that can hold up better in drought.

Do you see it? Look closely. At the base of the plant, a pipe drips water steadily to ensure proper irrigation.

When the climate goes crazy . . .

The tornado left little standing after it passed through Osceola County, Florida. In a richer country like the United States, people rebuild and resume normal life more rapidly than they do in countries with few disaster relief resources.

The 1990s were the hottest decade in the world since temperature records were kept. And 2001 and 2002? More of the same!

Is this the result of a bombing campaign? No! How about an earthquake? Wrong again. In February 1998, a tornado roared across parts of Florida. Winds of over 175 miles per hour blew away roofs, trees, piers, walls—just about everything!

Scientists think the number of cyclones, floods, torrential rainfalls, droughts, and other weather catastrophes could increase in the coming decades. Why is that? Mainly because temperatures are rising throughout the world. And weather-related disasters don't just cause deaths and homelessness. They also affect the local economy by destroying factories and wrecking farms. It's even worse when these sorts of disasters strike poor countries, countries that have little money and resources to make recovery easier.

But if everyone in the world cooperates, we might be able to attack this problem. How? As a start, those who live in industrialized nations could reduce their energy consumption, thus slowing down the process of global warming. It's a long, hard road, but one that the world needs to travel.

Look out—rising water!

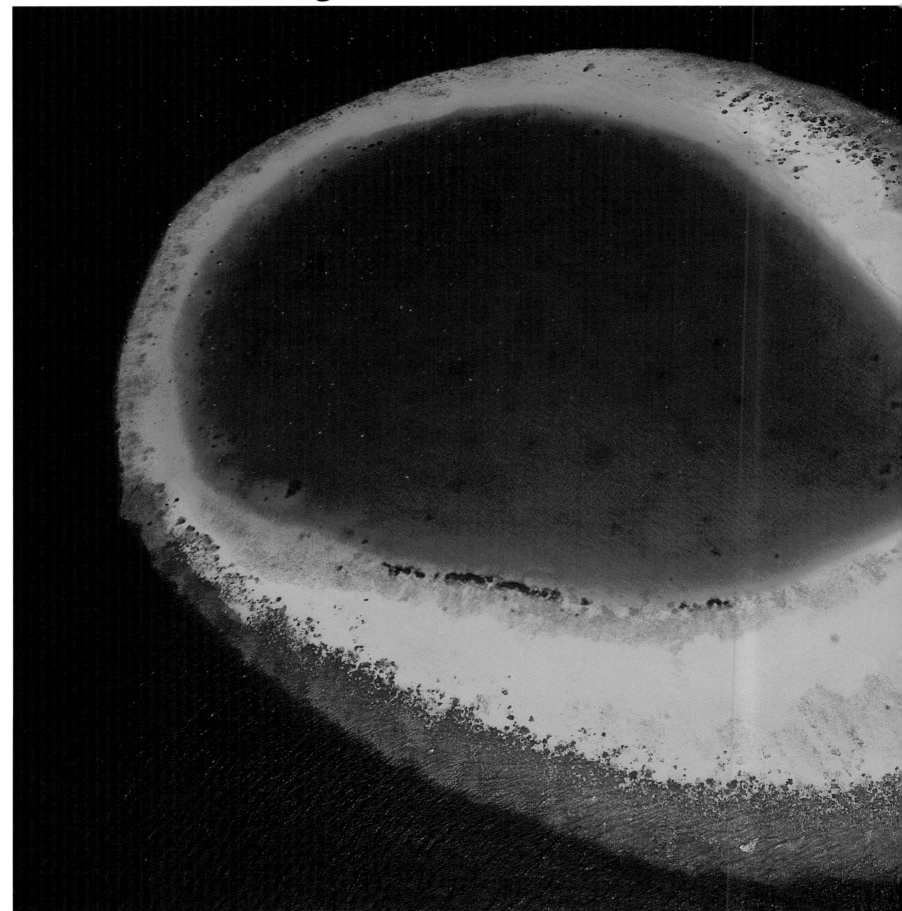

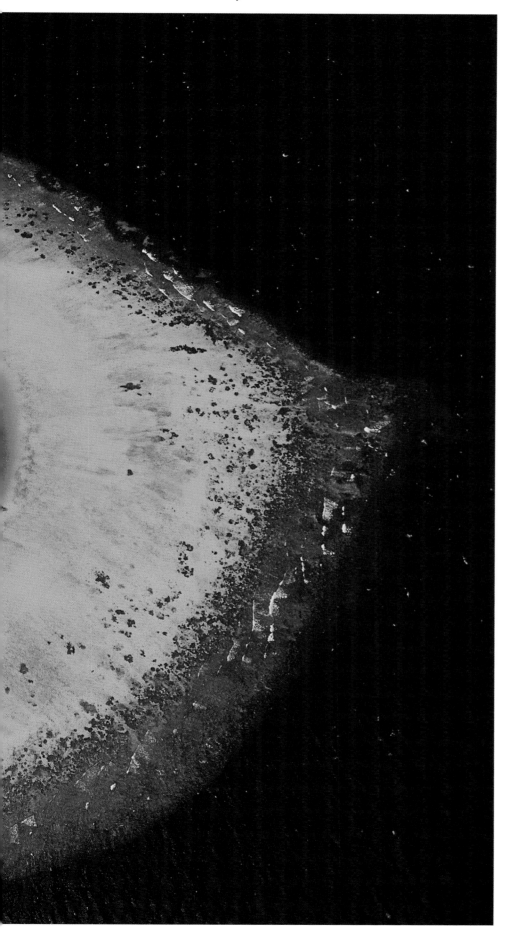

This is the eye of the Maldives on North Male Atoll. The brownish-green fringe bordering the sand beach is a coral reef. The highest point in the Maldives Islands reaches only about 8 feet above sea level.

If sea levels rise as much as three feet over the next few decades, 6% of the Netherlands and 17% of Bangladesh may be submerged underwater.

It looks like a gigantic blue eye staring into space, doesn't it? But with a few palm trees here and there, this tiny deserted island would become a paradise. Beneath the water, multicolored coral and fish abound. We're in the Maldives Islands in the Indian Ocean.

There are nearly 1,200 islands in the Maldives, and most of them barely break the ocean's surface. Thousands of similar islands, such as the Marshall and the Nauru, dot the Pacific Ocean. Many are inhabited right now—but their future is uncertain. Higher temperatures throughout the world will likely cause sea levels to rise, covering a large part of these islands. The people living there will have to move—but where? Moving will almost certainly cause both political and psychological problems. Tourism, too, will suffer, as will the colonies of seabirds and the rare sea turtles that also live there.

In 2001, representatives from the small Pacific islands met to develop strategies to prevent the sea from covering the islands. Some islands will have to build dikes to keep out the water. But whether this will help in the long run—only time will tell.

When the sea rises

Since the start of the twentieth century, the global temperature has risen by over 1 degree F and has increased at an even more rapid rate since the 1970s. This change also affects the ocean water. Think: what does water in a saucepan do when it heats up? It overflows! In the oceans, too, increased temperatures make water expand. In fact, the water level around the world could rise up to twenty inches in the next one hundred years. That's why some low coastlands (where many people often live) and flat islands may eventually be under the sea.

Shantytowns spread misery across the land

The city of Guayaquil, which has the largest population in Ecuador with 2 million residents, is ringed with shantytowns. Throughout the world, one million people move to cities each week.

In 1950, 70% of the world's population lived in the countryside. By 2025, 60% will live in cities.

Out and out and out. As far as you can see, the area around Guayaquil, Ecuador's principal trading port, is plastered with these small shanties, or ramshackle huts. The *barrios miserias* (poor neighborhoods) sprout on the smallest plots of useless land. These precarious "shantytowns" stand on marshy areas at the edge of the sea, where each tide throws up on shore its load of filth and refuse. The people live without schooling, without comforts, without safety, and without hygiene.

In many developing nations, people are flocking to the cities as their small farms disappear. Here is the main reason why. The crops these farmers once sold now compete with foreign products, and the farmers can no longer earn income. Large international companies, which can afford to export produce (in the case of Ecuador, fruits), now farm the land. As long as a decent life is impossible in the countryside, major cities will continue to attract the poorest, like a trap.

Is there any solution? New agricultural trade practices might offer a glimmer of hope. Such new practices will be difficult to put in place, but they could enable farmers to stay on their land and still earn enough to live.

An inland sea dries up

An old trawler lies beached in a desert in the Aralsk region, in Kazakhstan. Forty years ago, the Aral Sea reached this point. But now, the Sea is located more than thirty-five miles away!

In forty years, the Aral Sea has lost three-quarters of its water volume and one-half of its surface area.

Right now, this boat isn't going anywhere, is it? But just a few years ago, it was sailing in the Aral Sea. Located in Central Asia, the Aral was the fourth largest lake in the world. Two rivers, the Amu Darya and the Syr Darya, flowed into its slightly salty waters. But during the 1960s, the local government tried to transform the region's prairies into vast cotton fields. Irrigating these croplands took a lot of water, so engineers built canals to divert the rivers.

Can you guess what happened next? That's right: the Aral's water level fell. At the same time, because fresh water no longer flowed into the lake, the sea became saltier and saltier. Little by little, the salt scattered by winds burned off the nearby vegetation and made the land more sterile. Farming became difficult. Fish in the huge lake could not survive. Fishermen had to abandon their trade. The chain of catastrophe grew: the wind even carried salt from the Aral to the mountains of Tajikistan, where it penetrated the snow and speeded melting.

Yes, the government wanted to create cotton fields to generate wealth for the area. Instead, using this massive engineering project to disrupt the rivers' flow caused the region to sink into ruin.

Variety is the truth of life

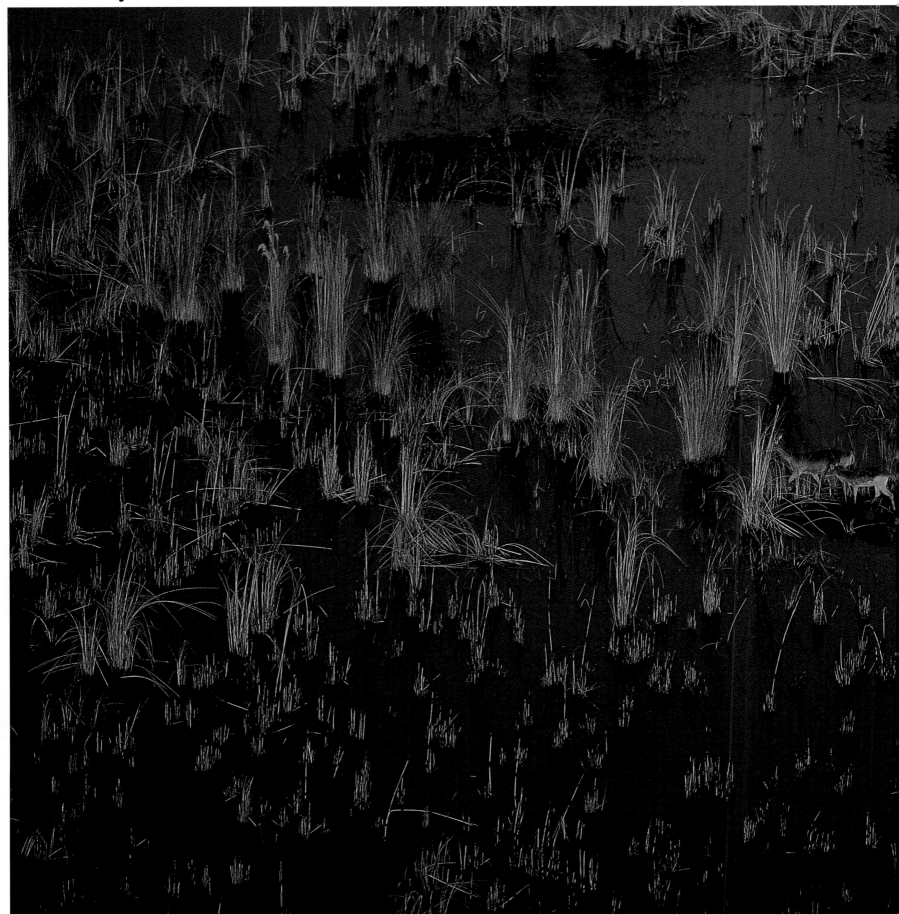

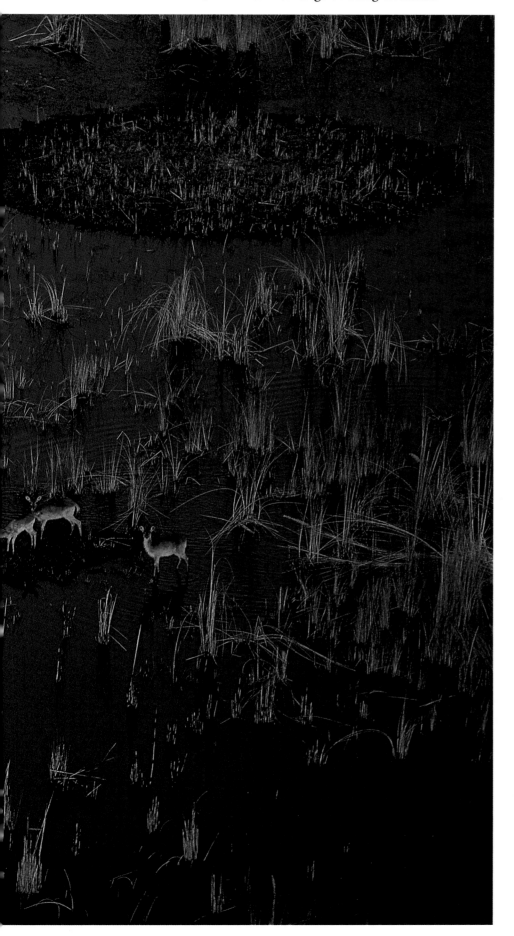

Frozen at attention here in the Okavango Delta, these antelope are attracted only to this type of marsh. These wet regions, which extend over nine thousand square miles, harbor a wide range of living creatures.

In just a few decades, human activities have seriously threatened the biodiversity that existed and evolved for over 3 billion years.

If you look very carefully, you'll see the antelope staring up at us. Do you see them? They're almost the same color as the marsh grasses, aren't they? On any summer hike across a meadow, a naturalist may see and identify hundreds of species, and be able to name each animal and plant.

But in some areas of the world this task is not so easy. Even on a single tree in a Peruvian forest, one naturalist counted more than 650 species of coleoptera (beetles)! So far, naturalists and scientists have counted 1,750,000 animal and plant species. Sounds like a lot, doesn't it? Yet this number could climb as high as 14 million species. What wonderful discoveries may lie ahead!

We call the fact that many different species live in a particular natural environment "biodiversity." The rich biodiversity on our planet is the result of many millions of years of slow evolution.

Every animal and plant has its place and role in the habitat where it lives. But the present-day destruction of natural environments is reducing biodiversity. So what? Well, this decreased biodiversity may eventually cause a major ecological disaster. That's because all species are linked to each other. Like a house of cards falling, when one habitat disappears, hundreds of species can be lost.

Thousands of species threatened

Did you know that currently more than 12,000 species of plants and animals are threatened with extinction? Some estimate that as many as 5,000 to 10,000 species vanish from the planet each year—that's a rate of one species per hour! Some people have tried to enact laws to protect endangered species, such as the rhinoceros. But how many other species we haven't yet discovered will disappear before we even get to know them?

A delicate balance between earth and sea . . .

In the Venice Lagoon, the sea meets the land to form small islands, which appear or disappear underwater, depending on the season. These areas provide rich environments for plants and animals.

Since 1930, plants that impede erosion have become increasingly scarce in the Venice Lagoon, speeding up the lagoon's deterioration.

As ocean temperatures rise, some low-lying land areas could be engulfed before too much longer. This means that cities like Venice, New York, and Tokyo could end up with their feet, so to speak, dangling in the water!

For Venice, the problem is coming sooner than later. From above, it looks like a giant jigsaw puzzle, doesn't it? But this beautiful lagoon of intertwined canals is gradually being covered with water as the sea extends over the land. And Venice is built on subsoil composed of clay and silt, so the city is slowly sinking. What's more, enlarging the channels and canals to make room for large boat traffic is only making the situation worse. At the same time, disturbing the soil with industrial projects and pumping underground water further weaken the substrata and increase erosion.

In the past few years, frequent floods have destroyed aquatic life and eaten away at the city's monuments. The Venetians need to find a way to save their amazing city without disrupting the lagoon's natural balance. They have started the "Moses" Project, which will construct hinged barriers on the seabed that will block the rising waters. No doubt about it, this is a good beginning. But unless people address the larger causes, the problems, like the water, will continue to rise.

Learning to think of the future

This map, which students painted in the schoolyard of a high school in France, reminds us that sustainable development concerns not only each citizen, but national governments as well. In 2002, the fifteen nations of the European Union ratified the Kyoto Protocol on climate change. This agreement binds them to reduce emissions of greenhouse gases by 8% from 1990 levels by the year 2012. So far, the United States has not ratified the agreement.

More than eight of ten children around the world go to school. This is progress, even though many of these young students have to miss school for long periods so they can work.

A man born one hundred years ago didn't believe that his wife had the same rights as he had. Today, in many countries, it's a fact that is clear to all. Just as a person changes as he lives his life, humanity learns and changes over time.

In our time, Earth's problems are forcing us to think and act differently. Knowledge is the most effective tool for transforming the world. New ways of thinking, and especially of acting, are open to someone who understands that throwing out wooden chopsticks after every meal in Tokyo or buying teak furniture in London uses up forestland in Indonesia or Brazil.

The world of human culture is a treasure. But the natural world is just as important. No one would think of destroying the books in a library. Why, then, would a person want to pick an endangered flower when he or she understands how rare the flower is?

Education throughout the world

Worldwide, one of four children between the ages of five and fourteen and one of five adults don't know how to read and write. This is especially true in Africa and Asia, but illiteracy exists in developed countries, too. Ask yourself: how can someone be an effective citizen without knowing how to read and write? To give everyone access to education by the year 2015 would require an investment of around $6 billion per year. It sounds like a lot of money, doesn't it? But it's just a drop in the bucket when one compares it to the $750 billion countries spend each year on weapons of war.

Drowning in garbage . . .

Mexico City produces almost twenty thousand tons of garbage daily. Its poorest citizens pick through the garbage to recover anything they can use again. A new town, named Chalco, has even grown up around the dump!

Over a lifetime, one person living in an industrialized country will consume more and generate more pollution than thirty to fifty residents of a developing country.

Do you see the person standing in the middle of all the garbage? Here's a hint—she's wearing a yellow hat! And here's a pretty amazing statistic: in industrialized nations, the amount of garbage a family creates has tripled in the past twenty years. Today, many dumps like this one exist throughout the world. Dumps pollute not only the air, but also the land and the groundwater beneath. Incineration (burning the garbage) doesn't really help either, because it releases dioxin, a potentially cancer-causing pollutant.

In fact, there is so much garbage that we have had to think up other solutions to deal with it. Today, we can recycle glass, paper, plastic, and metals and use them to make new things. Recycling helps us avoid throwing garbage away, and at the same time it saves raw materials, such as trees. People sort their garbage, and towns set up collection and recycling programs. Does your town have a recycling program?

Only wealthy countries have the means to prevent the pile-up of garbage mountains. In such countries, garbage treatment is now a major industry. Perhaps eventually we'll return to the days when we threw less away. Sooner or later, we'll have to become different kinds of consumers— consumers who buy more long-lasting products wrapped in less useless packaging.

Giant melting icebergs glide through the sea

These icebergs are floating slowly in the open sea off the coast of Antarctica. Only 10% to 20% of an iceberg's mass is visible; the rest lies beneath the water.

It's a fact: the continent of Antarctica holds 70% of all fresh water reserves on the planet.

B-r-r-r-r-r-r! It's chilly! Off the Adélie Coast, in Antarctica, sailors must be especially vigilant. Enormous icebergs drift in the ocean. That's because every so often, icebergs break away from the ice sheet that covers the pole. In the past few years, though, these icebergs have grown unbelievably large as bigger and bigger pieces of the ice sheet break away. Could this be happening in response to recent climate changes?

In March 2000, an iceberg split off from the Ross ice shelf in Antarctica. It was approximately 25 miles wide and 170 miles long, an area about the size of Connecticut. A gigantic iceberg like this gradually breaks apart, and ends by melting completely. But such icebergs have no real effect on the ocean's rise. An ice cube melting in a glass, for example, doesn't raise the level of the water in which it floats.

The icebergs' fragmentation prevents some species of penguins from feeding. How? By changing the winds and ocean currents, it drives the penguins' prey farther away from their colonies. But for other penguin species, the iceberg breakdown is a windfall: it is precisely in this kind of shelf, broken into a thousand pieces, that they find their food. So disrupting a particular habitat may have different effects on different species.

By removing ice samples and analyzing concentrations of carbon dioxide encased in the ice, scientists can learn about the history of the earth's climate.

Health care—for whom?

On the banks of the Chari River, in Chad, these colorful carpets drying in the sun look harmless. But they're being washed in the same water used for personal washing, drinking, and cooking. Using the water for so many purposes increases the risk of disease.

Every day around the world, more than thirty thousand children die from diseases for which they could easily be treated.

In some countries, health care, like education, is considered a public service governments provide for their citizens. Most people are vaccinated against infectious diseases, treated when they're ill, and informed about preventing health problems. The average American lives into her or his later seventies. But in Bangladesh, life expectancy is sixty-three, while it's fifty in Haiti, forty-two in Afghanistan, and only thirty-four in Sierra Leone.

In fact, because many countries lack an effective health-care system, some preventable diseases still cause epidemics. Cholera is one such disease. A more serious disease, AIDS, has struck 40 million people—up to 28 million of whom live in sub-Saharan Africa. Although medicines may help the sick survive, the companies that make the medicines often charge such a high price that many sick people can't afford it.

Everyone agrees that good health is essential. Some charitable organizations now set up vaccination campaigns to help immunize the world's children against diseases which, when the resources are available, are always preventable. The tide seems to be slowly turning, but for many it still turns too late.

Living off the land . . .

In this region of Nepal, families grow rice on the mountainsides. 80% of the Nepalese people live off of traditional farming.

In Nepal, families live off their own land. In contrast, 1% of the major agricultural firms in Brazil own roughly half of Brazil's farmland.

Look closely. Do you see a family working in their fields? In many places, each individual family has a small patch of land on which to grow the cereals, fruits, and vegetables that feed it. This system is called traditional, or subsistence, farming. The family sells any surplus it grows in the local market. It's definitely a long way from the intensive, large-scale agriculture practiced in industrialized nations. And maybe that's a good thing, since these small-scale farmers use little water, small quantities of fuel for their machines, and few, or no, chemicals.

Monoculture (growing a single crop over vast areas) requires costly, polluting machines and chemicals. Traditional farming, on the other hand, uses small amounts of water and natural products, such as manure, to enrich the soil. Furthermore, mixed farming (growing different crops) is possible on tiny plots of land, so small individual landowners can do all the work. This type of farming gives greater yields, and the farmers are able to keep control of their tools and land. It may be that traditional agriculture, with its respect for the land and those who work it, holds promise for the future of developing countries.

A healthy diversity

Once upon a time, India had 200,000 varieties of rice. These included, for instance, one strain of rice whose stalks grew over fifteen feet high and which stood undaunted by flood. There was also rice that withstood drought and salt. Over hundreds of years, farmers had created varieties of rice suited to the local soil and climate. But since the 1950s, many varieties all over the globe have disappeared.

Traffic: smothering the world?

A highway interchange near Yokohama, Japan, seems to bind up the land with heavy ropes. Cars, it's true, are a highly practical means of transportation. But their increased presence in developed countries has also increased the amount of polluted air.

Exhaust from traffic accounts for one-quarter of all carbon dioxide (CO_2) emissions into the atmosphere.

Could you find your way through this maze of hoops and loops? Maybe not, but thousands of people drive here every day. People often live in one place and work in another, traveling by train, bus, or, most often, by car. Many goods we use also travel over long distances, whether made on the other side of the globe and sold here, or vice versa. Today, our way of life often depends on cars, even though they cost lots of money. Another cost is in time: many residents of big cities spend several hours a day on the road.

Above all, though, there's the cost in pollution. Airplanes, trucks, and the endless lines of cars emit carbon dioxide (CO_2), which is largely responsible for global warming. These vehicles produce other pollutants, too, which make city air dirty and hard to breathe. And that's not even considering the noise from automobile or airplane traffic!

How can we pollute less when we travel? Well, we can walk, take bicycles, or use mass transit! We can make this choice, when possible. On a larger scale, however, we can also transport goods differently. For instance, piggybacking, or placing trucks on trains, allows them to cross whole regions without using nearly as much fuel. But this is just a start!

Vital coastlines under siege . . .

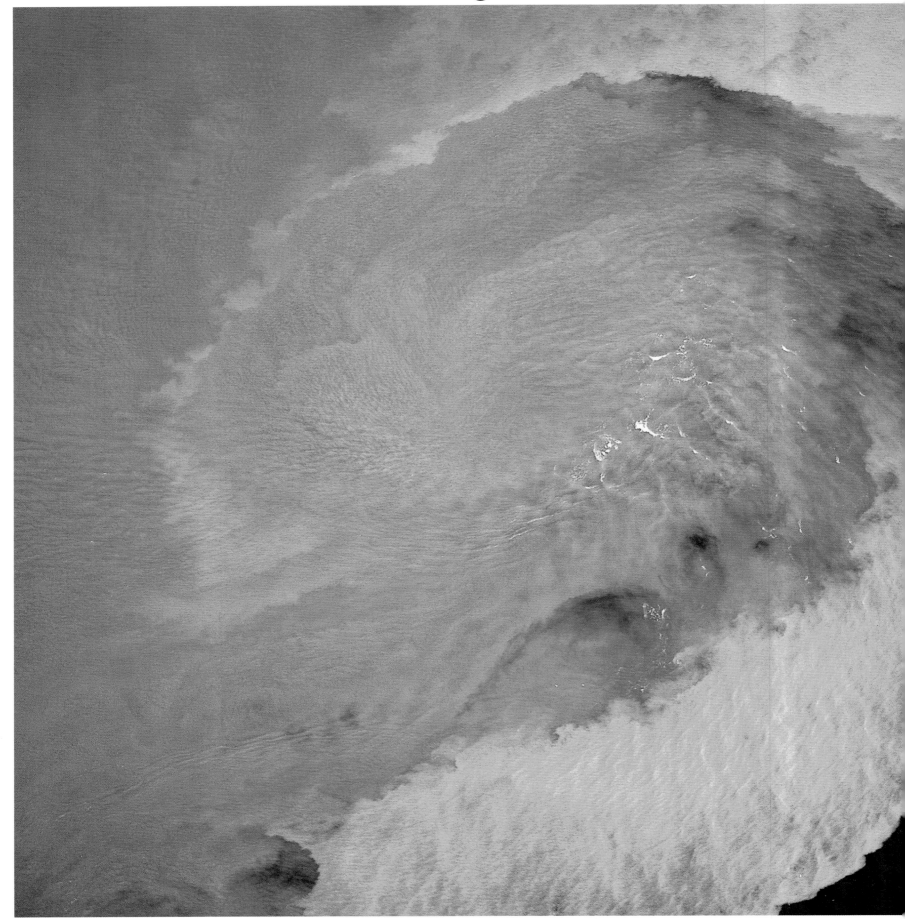

Mining gold deposits on the coast of the island of Mindanao, in the Philippines, produces waste discharges. Beneath these colored waters, the coral reefs are dying. They have been polluted and can absorb less of the light they need.

All over the world, nearly one of every four people lives less than forty miles from a coast.

At first glance, this looks like a beautiful, greenish-yellow swirl of color. In fact, however, it's water. Water, you might ask, that doesn't appear to be blue? One hundred years ago, there would have been no question at all: the sea here was uniformly blue. Today, though, goldmines operating on a nearby Philippine island discharge waste products that pollute the ocean and release sediment (fine particles ripped from the soil by water or wind) that disrupts ocean currents and destroys the balance of life in this place.

All over the world, ocean coastlines are vital to the health of our planet. Near many coastlines, fish lay their eggs. Tropical coasts shelter profusions of mangroves, which are forests with their roots in the sea. Growing between land and ocean, the mangroves shelter fish and birds. These small trees stop and anchor the advancing sediments and help stabilize the shorelines.

Disturbing these habitats can destroy the local animals and plants. It also can have a negative effect on tourism, through which many people find jobs and a decent income. Reasonable land use, waste-water treatment, and protecting rivers, beaches, reefs, and mangroves will conserve a unique environment.

Harnessing the wind

This windmill installation at Middelgrunden, off Copenhagen, is one of the largest such installations in Europe. It supplies 3% of the Danish capital's electricity. It also suggests the possibility of finding new ways to bring needed energy to people everywhere.

Around the world, the use of wind and solar power is growing. Their use has risen by 35% and 21%, respectively, since 1995.

What have we here? A strange, modern sculpture? No, not at all. This bizarre metal forest in the open sea is actually a windmill installation. Each windmill has a propeller that the wind turns, generating electricity. Do you think they're beautiful? Well, whether you think they're attractive or not, windmills don't harm the natural environment and don't seem to threaten the birds that must avoid them. And windmills are increasingly appearing in regions where wind flow is abundant.

It's true that most energy we use for transportation, energy, manufacturing, and heating still comes from fossil fuels such as petroleum. But the supply of these fuels is limited—and they also pollute. What then? We are learning how to harness clean, sustainable energy sources: sun, wind, and river water.

Along rivers, hydroelectric plants use the force of water to produce energy. In rural areas, small dams generate electricity at modest cost. In sunny areas, solar panels can capture the heat of the sun and change it into electricity for light and hot water. Many hope that these three solutions, in combination with others, will supply us with future renewable energy sources. But even so, we will still have to consume less energy than we do today.

The future is now!

Our planet's problems remind us that what each of us does affects the Earth's future and all of our lives together. This is good news, because our individual decisions matter—let alone the decisions of a company, a city, or an entire country! We can no longer do nothing. We have to act as one.

A few decades ago, people would divert a river to water a dry steppe. This is what happened with the Aral Sea, which has largely evaporated and brought ruin to an entire region. Today, we are searching for better ideas. Gradually we are inventing complex, often surprising, solutions that unite ancient know-how with advanced technologies. These solutions attempt to use nature—while respecting it.

Let's look at a few of them.

• Organic farming is farming in harmony with the environment. This kind of farming uses no chemicals, preserves woods and hedges, employs natural fertilizers, and maintains fallow land to avoid exhausting the soil. Many consumers are in favor of this farming method, because product quality is more important to them than quantity. And organic farmers can usually live decently, because their crop prices are somewhat higher. This is a good model for many farmers in industrialized nations.

• Nowadays, forests are no longer considered simply wood-producing factories. Responsible foresters avoid planting conifers and poplars everywhere, as they did not so long ago because these trees are fast growers. The choice

Cattle farming in France

of which trees to plant depends on the particular habitat and the climate changes that affect tree growth. In tropical regions, some new projects allow forest-dwelling people to refrain from resorting to uncontrolled land clearing for money, while at the same time they become guardians of forests preserved in national parks and reserves. And thanks to enlightened tourism, which respects local traditions, people are helping protect forests and encouraging forest dwellers to remain in their traditional environments.

A healthy forest in Canada

• In villages all over the globe, charitable organizations work with residents to improve living conditions. For example, these organizations build small clinics that train nurses on-site and install micro-power stations that run on solar power and bio-gas (gases generated from animal droppings) to supply electricity. They help develop effective crop-watering systems and select sturdy seeds for planting. They also set up a credit system that allows local people to borrow money at low interest rates, which can lead to the establishment of successful small businesses. All these solutions enable village residents to build a better future.

• Finally, here is an example of a link between nature conservation and social problems. Some groups are restoring farmlands by creating "organic vegetable gardens." The produce is sold to garden-basket subscribers. The gardeners are formerly unemployed people who have been retrained. It's a small step, perhaps, but it is still a good example of a partnership between productive work, an intelligent use of nature, and consumer commitment.

Ecologically harmonious living in Denmark

WORLDWIDE DISTRIBUTION OF WATER RESOURCES

GREENLAND
(Denmark)

ALASKA
(United States)

ICELAND

NORWAY SWEDE

DENMARK

IRELAND UNITED
KINGDOM

GERMANY P

BELGIUM

LUXEMBOURG

SWITZERLAND

FRANCE

CANADA

2

1 HU

4

5

ITALY

PORTUGAL

SPAIN

UNITED STATES

TUNISIA

MOROCCO

ALGERIA

L

MEXICO

CUBA

DOMINICAN
REPUBLIC

HAITI

MAURITANIA

MALI

NIGER

ATLANTIC
OCEAN

BELIZE

HONDURAS

GUATEMALA

EL SALVADOR

NICARAGUA

Sénégal

SENEGAL

GAMBIA

GUINEA
BISSAU

Niger

BURKINA
FASO

GUINEA

GHANA

TOGO

BENIN

NIGERIA

SIERRA
LEONE

IVORY
COAST

COSTA RICA

PACIFIC
OCEAN

PANAMA

VENEZUELA

GUYANA

SURINAME

FRENCH GUIANA

LIBERIA

COLOMBIA

CAMEROON

EQUATORIAL
GUINEA

CON

GABON

ECUADOR

Amazon

Countries not indicated
on the map:

1. AUSTRIA
2. CZECH REPUBLIC
3. SLOVAKIA
4. SLOVENIA
5. CROATIA
6. BOSNIA-HERZEGOVINA
7. SERBIA-MONTENEGRO
8. MACEDONIA
9. ALBANIA
10. MOLDOVA

PERU

BRAZIL

Tocantins

São Francisco

BOLIVIA

Paraná

ANG

NAM

Cartography by Noël Meunier

PARAGUAY

Fresh Water Resources
Renewable Water Resources in 2000
(in approximate cubic feet/person/year)

URUGUAY

0	300	1500	5000	15000

ARGENTINA

CHILE

Countries in which the majority of the
population have no access to a well or
spring that provides drinkable water.

Countries in which the water resources
are decreasing due to overuse.

Water-related conflicts

◎ Major conflicts between states arising
from the use of river waters

Sources: WHO, UN, WRI